MEL BAY'S DELUXE
BLUEGRASS FLATPICKIN' GUITAR METHOD

By Neil & Steve Griffin

A COMPLETE STUDY INTO EVERY FACET OF BLUEGRASS GUITAR IN THE FLAT-PICKING STYLE.

INCLUDES:

1 2 3 4 5 6 7 8 9 0

DELUXE BLUEGRASS / FLAT-PICKING GUITAR METHOD

The Authors: Neil Griffin and Steve Griffin — performing musicians, band leaders and co-owners of The Neil Griffin Studios of Music located in Charlotte, North Carolina, where this method has been field tested and proven with students of all ages.

A WORD ABOUT THIS METHOD FROM THE AUTHORS

We have attempted to set forth a basic "From the Beginning" system of flat-picking guitar instruction for the use of both teachers and students.

Through the use of this method, the student should expect to learn the following:

1. How to pick out tunes single string style. (one note at a time)
2. How to play chord accompaniment.
3. How to play full Bluegrass flat-picking solos with melody and chords mixed together.

All the songs and solos in this book are written in two simple keys — G and C. All the playing is done in the basic position. (the first few frets)

The student will learn to play slides, hammers, and pull-offs — the three effects that are used so much in Bluegrass playing.

All of the songs in the solo section, except the fiddle type tunes, are written two ways: one simple version showing the single note melody as well as the chords and words; and one complete flat-picking solo that matches. If you have a friend who plays a few chords on the guitar or any other instrument, it will be fun to play the songs with him, swapping back and forth with one playing the melody and the other strumming the chords. Later when you can handle full solos, the music will still work together.

Daily practice is essential in order to master the material in this method and is one thing you must discipline yourself to do. No one else can do it for you.

Good luck and above all have fun with your music!

PARTS OF THE GUITAR

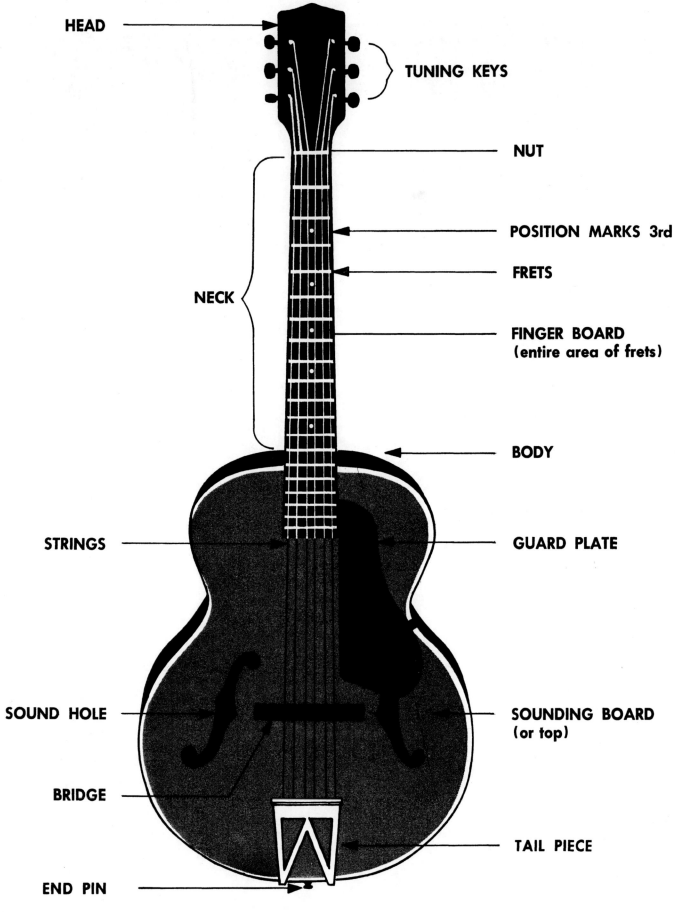

HEAD

TUNING KEYS

NUT

POSITION MARKS 3rd

FRETS

NECK

FINGER BOARD
(entire area of frets)

BODY

STRINGS

GUARD PLATE

SOUND HOLE

SOUNDING BOARD
(or top)

BRIDGE

TAIL PIECE

END PIN

HOLDING THE GUITAR

THIS IS THE PICK

HOLD IT IN THIS MANNER
FIRMLY BETWEEN THE THUMB
AND FIRST FINGER.

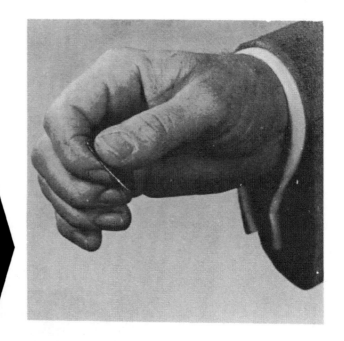

THE LEFT HAND POSITION

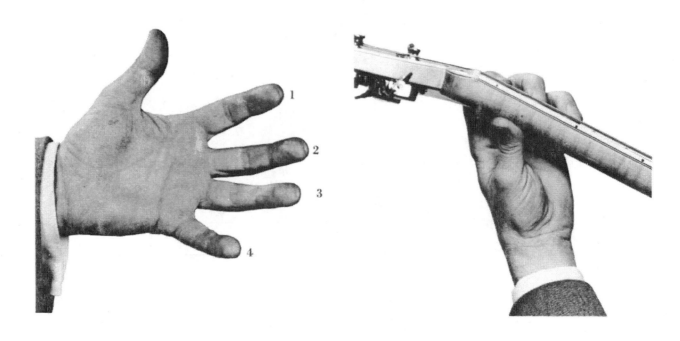

Place your fingers FIRMLY on the strings DIRECTLY BEHIND THE FRETS.

MUSIC READING SECTION

THIS SECTION INCLUDES THE FOLLOWING:

THE BASIC RUDIMENTS OF MUSIC

TUNING THE GUITAR

READING TABLATURE

TIME AND COUNTING IN MUSIC
AND TABLATURE

ALL NOTES IN THE BASIC
OR OPEN POSITION

BASIC CHORDS

CHORD STRUMMING

MANY SIMPLE SONGS TO PICK
AND CHORD

BASS RUNS

SOLO PLAYING—MELODY AND
CHORDS TOGETHER

THE QUICKEST WAY TO LEARN TO PLAY THE GUITAR BY "EAR" IS BY READING NOTES!

That sounds like a crazy statement doesn't it? It isn't, because when you think about it, in order for anyone to play an instrument by "ear" they must know where the different pitches and sounds are on that instrument. The quickest way to learn where they are is to write them down and study them correctly instead of "fishing" for them.

Those monsterous, mysterious, written musical notes that everyone seems so afraid of can be the greatest friend and helper you ever had when it comes to making music.

The musical alphabet has only seven letters—A, B, C, D, E, F, and G—with sharps and flats there are still only a total of twelve different notes. You can remember these as easy as you can twelve friends, twelve different kinds of automobiles, or even a couple of phone numbers. That doesn's sound so hard now does it?

Music notes are put together in different orders to produce different tunes just as letters are put together to produce words. You will learn where all the different sounds are on the guitar by reading the notes and listening to them. Before long your "ear" will be able to direct the fingers to the sounds you want and if you can sing or hum a tune you will be able to pick it out on the guitar.

The most important reason I can give you for learning to read notes is this—You will be able to pick up any piece of music and play the melody even if you have never heard it—This will make thousands of songs available to you without having to listen to them over and over trying to remember how they go.

TRY IT OUR WAY—YOU'LL GET THERE QUICKER!

NOTES VERSUS TABLATURE

It really isn't that way at all. Those who already can read tablature should be able to play the songs in this book, but if you are starting from the beginning let me urge you to use the note system as the most important and learn the tablature as a helper.

Tablature is necessary to show where to play notes when the same note can be played in two different places on the fingerboard—also it is easier to read when playing solos high on the neck but don't forget tablature is just a helper and not the best way to learn to play.

THE RUDIMENTS OF MUSIC

THE STAFF

Music is written on a STAFF consisting of FIVE LINES and FOUR SPACES.
The lines and spaces are numbered upward as shown:

5TH LINE ————————————————————————
4TH LINE ——————————————— 4TH SPACE ——————
3RD LINE ——————————————— 3RD SPACE ——————
2ND LINE ——————————————— 2ND SPACE ——————
1ST LINE ——————————————— 1ST SPACE ——————

THE LINES AND SPACES ARE NAMED AFTER LETTERS OF THE ALPHABET.

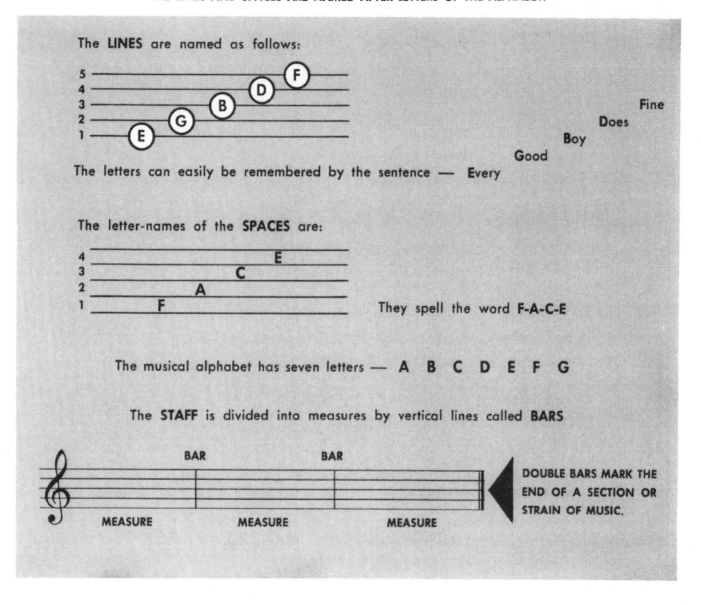

The **LINES** are named as follows:

The letters can easily be remembered by the sentence — Every Good Boy Does Fine

The letter-names of the **SPACES** are:

They spell the word F-A-C-E

The musical alphabet has seven letters — A B C D E F G

The **STAFF** is divided into measures by vertical lines called **BARS**

BAR   BAR

MEASURE   MEASURE   MEASURE

DOUBLE BARS MARK THE END OF A SECTION OR STRAIN OF MUSIC.

THE CLEF

THIS SIGN IS THE TREBLE OR G CLEF.

ALL GUITAR MUSIC WILL BE WRITTEN IN THIS CLEF.

THE SECOND LINE OF THE TREBLE CLEF IS KNOWN AS THE G LINE. MANY PEOPLE CALL THE TREBLE CLEF THE G CLEF BECAUSE IT CIRCLES AROUND THE G LINE.

OTHER MUSICAL SIGNS AND TERMS

The Repeat

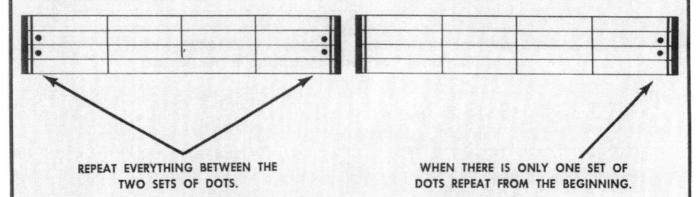

REPEAT EVERYTHING BETWEEN THE
TWO SETS OF DOTS.

WHEN THERE IS ONLY ONE SET OF
DOTS REPEAT FROM THE BEGINNING.

The Accent

The accent mark (>) above or below a note indicates that you are to pick that note harder. Example

Some Musical Terms And What They Mean

D. C. — means go back to the beginning.

D. S. — means go back to the sign (𝄋) wherever it is placed in the music.

AL — means play down to.

FINE — means the end, or to stop wherever the word "Fine" is placed in the music.

To CODA — the Coda (⊕) is an extra or final ending to a piece of music.

EXAMPLES OF ABOVE

D. C. al Fine — means go back to the beginning and play down to the word "Fine".

D. S. al Fine — means go back to the sign (𝄋) and play down to the word "Fine".

D. C. al Coda — means go back to the beginning and play down to where it says to Coda or ⊕ and then jump down to the Coda ⊕ for the final ending.

1st and 2nd endings

It is sometimes necessary to play a song or section of a song through twice, ending it differently Each time- this is accomplished by writing 2 separate endings and numbering them 1 and 2 as shown below.

play 1st time only   play 2nd time only

VOLUME MARKINGS

The following markings indicate how loud or soft to play.

pp—very soft

p—soft

mp—medium soft

mf—medium loud

f—very loud

SPEED MARKINGS

ritard—slow down

a tempo—go back to original speed

accelerando—get faster

Andante—slow

Allegro—fast

TUNING THE GUITAR

The six open strings of the guitar will be of the same pitch as the six notes shown in the illustration of the piano keyboard. Note that five of the strings are below the middle C of the piano keyboard.

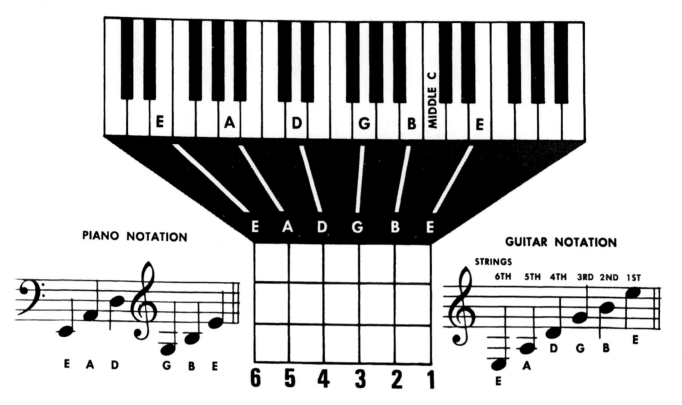

PIANO NOTATION

GUITAR NOTATION

ANOTHER METHOD OF TUNING

1. Tune the 6th string in unison to the **E** or twelfth white key to the LEFT of MIDDLE C on the piano.

2. Place the finger behind the fifth fret of the 6th string. This will give you the tone or pitch of the 5th string. (**A**)

3. Place finger behind the fifth fret of the 5th string to get the pitch of the 4th string. (**D**)

4. Repeat same procedure to obtain the pitch of the 3rd string. (**G**)

5. Place finger behind the FOURTH FRET of the 3rd string to get the pitch of the 2nd string. (**B**)

6. Place finger behind the fifth fret of the 2nd string to get the pitch of the 1st string. (**E**)

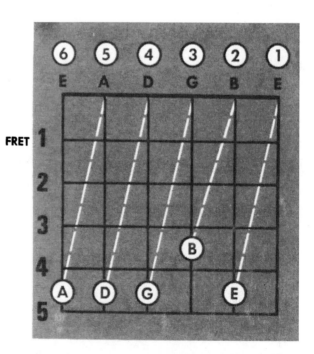

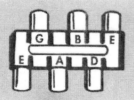

PITCH PIPES

Pitch pipes with instructions for their usage may be obtained at any music store. Each pipe will have the correct pitch of each guitar string and are recommended to be used when a piano is not available.

READING TABLATURE

Tablature is simply a drawing of the 6 strings of the guitar with numbers showing you to-either pick a string open or in which fret to press a string down to produce the note called for in the music.

The tablature will appear throughout this book directly under each note of music showing which string and in which fret every note is found on the guitar.

Shown below are examples of tablature with an explanation of each item.

There are six lines in the tablature, one for each string on the guitar as shown above.

The numbers placed on the tablature lines show in which fret to press down the left hand fingers.

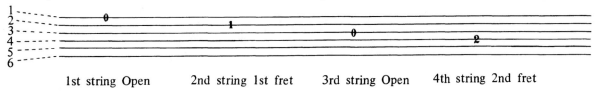

1st string Open   2nd string 1st fret   3rd string Open   4th string 2nd fret

When two or more notes are played at the same time, the numbers are above one another as shown below.

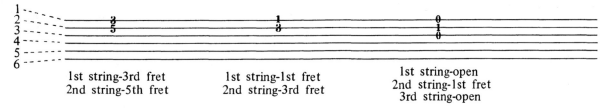

1st string-3rd fret
2nd string-5th fret

1st string-1st fret
2nd string-3rd fret

1st string-open
2nd string-1st fret
3rd string-open

NOTES ON THE "E" OR 1ST STRING

E	F	G
OPEN STRING	1st FINGER - 1st FRET	3rd FINGER - 3rd FRET

Pick each note evenly and say the names of the notes out loud as you play. This will help in learning them quicker.

PLAYING ON THE 1st STRING

NOTES ON THE "B" OR 2ND STRING

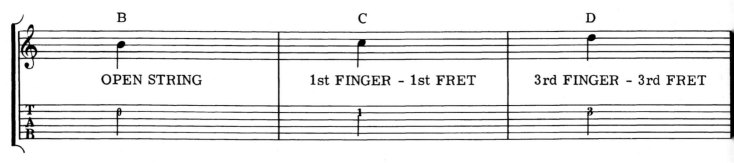

B	C	D
OPEN STRING	1st FINGER - 1st FRET	3rd FINGER - 3rd FRET

PLAYING ON THE 2nd STRING

NOTE CHART

Below is a complete chart of the six notes you have learned. The notes are shown going up and then back down. You should practice playing these notes and naming them out loud at least ten times each day until you have memorized them!

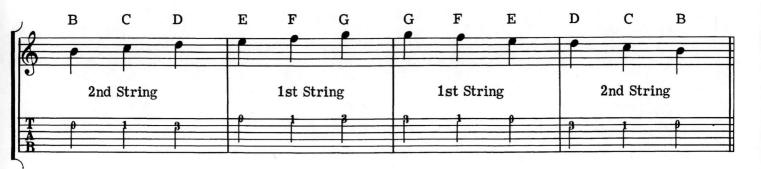

MIXING THE NOTES

TIME VALUES OF NOTES AND RESTS

The shape (construction) of notes tell you how long to let a note sound before playing the next note.

The shape (construction) of rests tell you how long to be silent before playing the next note.

The notes and rests you will use and their relationship to each other are shown below:

WHOLE NOTE	𝅝	WHOLE REST	4 COUNTS
DOTTED HALF NOTE	𝅗𝅥.	DOTTED HALF REST	3 COUNTS
HALF NOTE	𝅗𝅥	HALF REST	2 COUNTS
QUARTER NOTE	♩	QUARTER REST	1 COUNT
EIGHTH NOTE	♪	EIGHTH REST	1/2 COUNT
SIXTEENTH NOTE	𝅘𝅥𝅯	SIXTEENTH REST	1/4 COUNT

Note: Two eighth notes may be written ♪ ♪ or ♫

Two sixteenth notes may be written 𝅘𝅥𝅯 𝅘𝅥𝅯 or 𝅘𝅥𝅯𝅘𝅥𝅯

THE RULE OF THE DOTTED NOTE

A dot placed after a note makes the note longer by one-half of its original value:

Examples of dotted Notes:

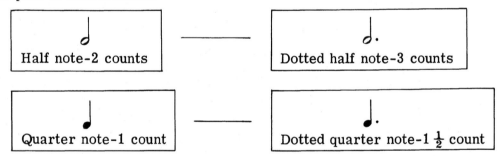

Half note-2 counts	—	Dotted half note-3 counts
Quarter note-1 count	—	Dotted quarter note-1 ½ count

THE TIED NOTE

Two notes of the same musical pitch (two G'S, two B's etc.) may be tied together with a curved line. This creates one note equal to the total value of both. Remember pick the note only once and hold it for the total value of both notes.

Examples of tied notes:

2 + 1 = 3

4 + 2 = 6

4 + 1 = 5

1 + ½ = 1 ½

14

THE TIME SIGNATURE

At the beginning of each piece of music is set two numbers that tell you the total number of counts in each measure of the music and the type of note that receives one count.

This is called the "time signature" : The top number is the number of counts in each measure and the bottom number is the kind of note that gets one count.

Examples of time signatures:

$\dfrac{4}{4}$ = Four counts per measure
a quarter note ($\quarternote$) gets one count

$\dfrac{3}{4}$ = Three counts per measure
a quarter note ($\quarternote$) gets one count

$\dfrac{2}{4}$ = Two counts per measure
a quarter note ($\quarternote$) gets one count

There are other time signatures but the three shown and explained above will be the ones most used in guitar picking.

Keeping steady time is the most important part of playing any musical instrument. You must, from the very beginning, learn to keep a steady beat or count when you play.

Try the following:
Tap your foot on the floor at a steady pace slowly and evenly at a speed that sounds like someone walking slowly along at an even pace.

For $\frac{4}{4}$ time practice over and over tapping your foot with each count-(1-2-3-4), (1-2-3-4), etc.

For $\frac{3}{4}$ time count-(1-2-3), (1-2-3); etc.

For $\frac{2}{4}$ time count-(1-2), (1-2), etc.

Practice counting in the three time signatures above, keeping steady time by tapping the foot or by clapping your hands together. Remember each count must be given the same amount of time.

You can never play the guitar well unless you learn to keep steady time so WORK AT IT every time you pick up your instrument, THIS IS VERY IMPORTANT!

COUNTING TIME IN TABLATURE

Counting time in tablature will be exactly the same as in regular musical notation, using a time signature at the beginning, with measures separated by bar lines, and with stems being used for the different time values.

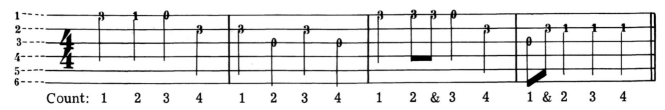

Count: 1 2 3 4   1 2 3 4   1 2 & 3 4   1 & 2 3 4

The only difference in tablature counting will be that if a note is to be held longer than one count, it will be shown as follows:

The first count will have the regular quarter note stem and will be connected to one additional quarter note stem for each additional count the note is to be held.

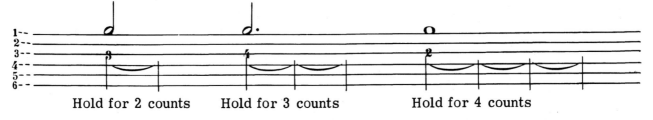

Hold for 2 counts   Hold for 3 counts   Hold for 4 counts

Although you may know how to read standard notation, it will be helpful to refer to the tablature to make sure notes are played in the best playing position.

NOTE: THE STUDENT IS NOT EXPECTED TO UNDERSTAND ALL OF THE ABOVE IMFORMATION UNTIL HE HAS STUDIED THE FOLLOWING SECTIONS OF THIS BOOK:

TIME VALUES OF NOTES AND RESTS

THE TIME SIGNATURE

COUNTING

COUNTING TIME

It is very important the student count out loud while playing the following exercises, saying the numbers written under the notes. As explained before, a "steady" pace must be used.

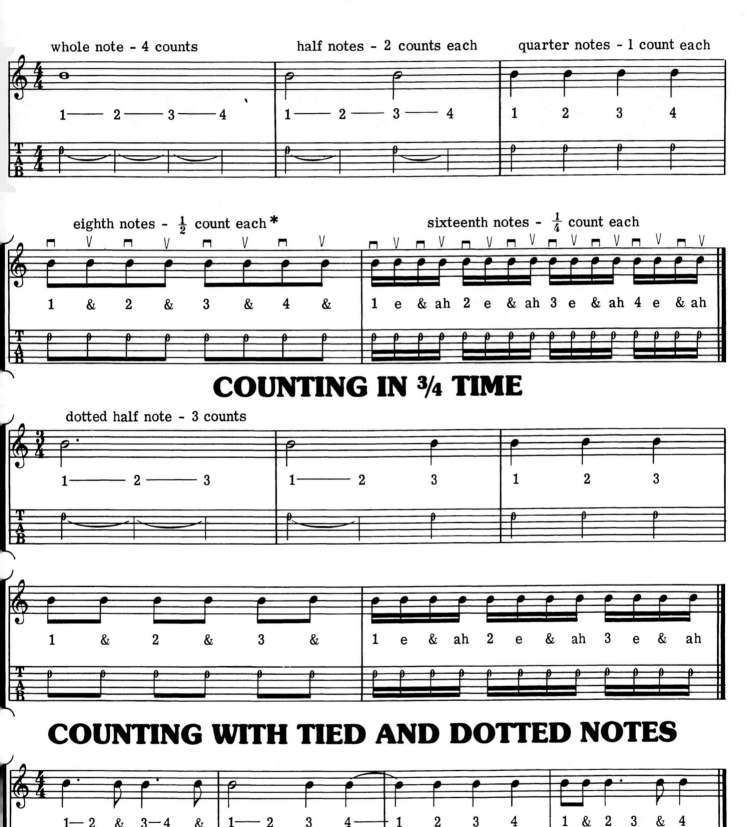

whole note - 4 counts

half notes - 2 counts each

quarter notes - 1 count each

eighth notes - $\frac{1}{2}$ count each *

sixteenth notes - $\frac{1}{4}$ count each

COUNTING IN ¾ TIME

dotted half note - 3 counts

COUNTING WITH TIED AND DOTTED NOTES

* Pick: Down (⊓) and Up (∨)

17

BILE' DEM CABBAGE DOWN

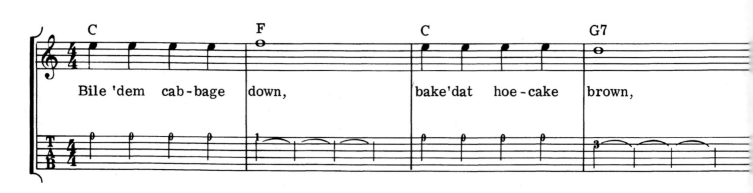

Bile 'dem cab-bage down, bake'dat hoe-cake brown,

on-ly song I e-ver sing is Bile 'dem cab-bage down._____

Play chords the first time thru
Play tablature the 2nd time thru

MERRILY WE PICK ALONG

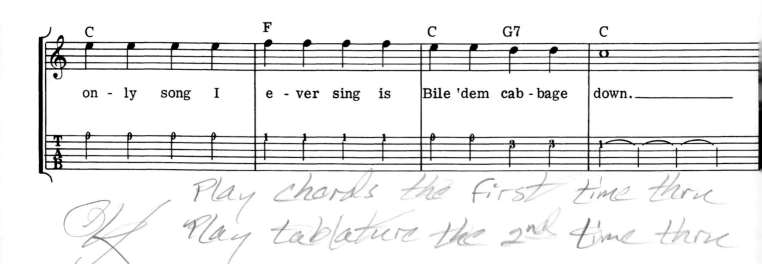

Mer-ri-ly we pick a-long, pick a-long, pick a-long,

Bass strum Brush strum B S B S B S B S B S B S

small *large*

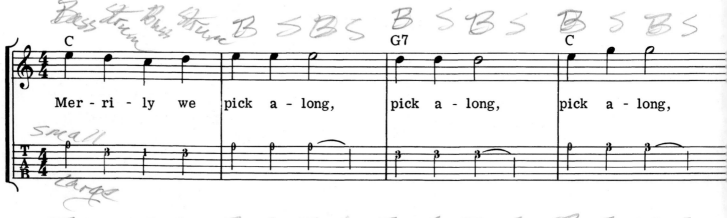

B S B S B S B S B S B S B S B S

mer-ri-ly we pick a-long, on the old gui-tar._____

SHOO FLY

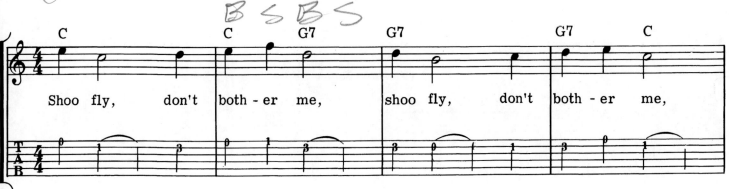

Shoo fly, don't both-er me, shoo fly, don't both-er me,

shoo fly, don't both-er me, Oh, go somewhere that I'll not be.

SKIP TO MY LOU

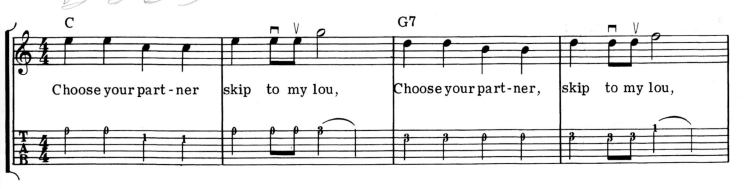

Choose your part-ner skip to my lou, Choose your part-ner, skip to my lou,

Choose your part-ner, skip to my lou, Skip to my lou, My dar - - lin'.

NOTES ON THE "G" OR 3RD STRING

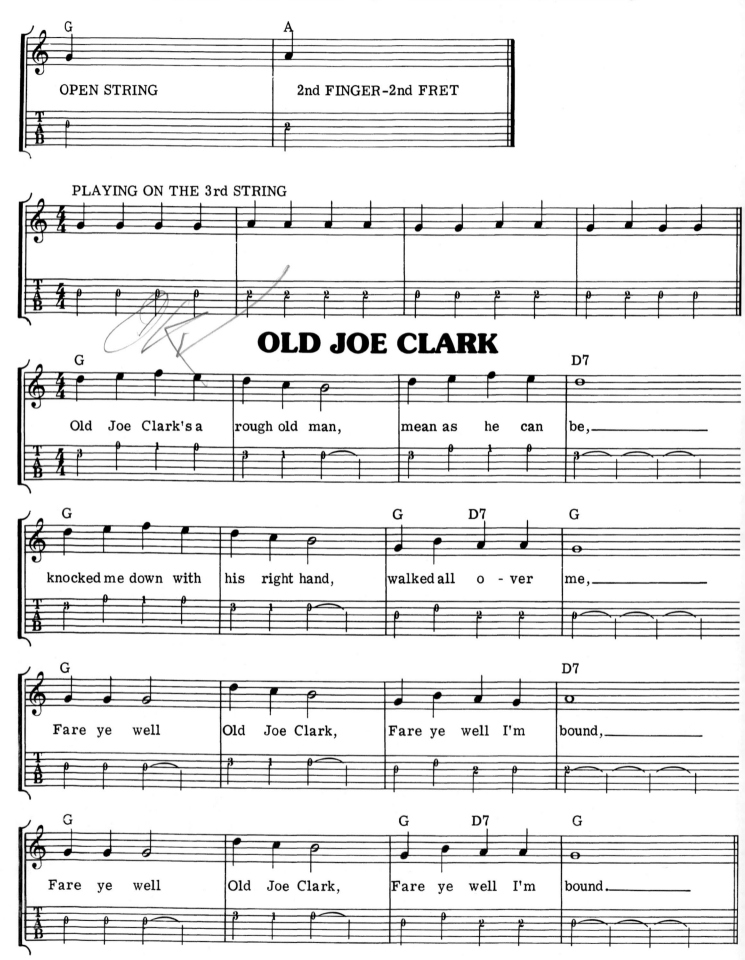

OLD JOE CLARK

Old Joe Clark's a rough old man, mean as he can be,

knocked me down with his right hand, walked all o - ver me,

Fare ye well Old Joe Clark, Fare ye well I'm bound,

Fare ye well Old Joe Clark, Fare ye well I'm bound.

FRENCH SONG

RED RIVER VALLEY

CRIPPLE CREEK

Goin' up crip-ple creek | Goin' on a run, | Goin' up crip-ple creek to | have some fun,

Goin' up crip-ple creek, | Goin' on a run, | Goin' up crip-ple creek to | have some fun.

OLD MacDONALD

Old Mac Don - ald | had a farm | E - I - E - I | O and

on that farm he | had some ducks | E - I E - I - | O with a

quack quack here and a | quack quack there | here a quack there a quack | every where a quack quack

Old Mac Don - ald | had a farm | E - I E - I | O.

22

NOTES ON THE "D" OR 4TH STRING

NOTE CHART

Below is a chart of all the notes you have learned - practice daily.

I WISH I WAS SINGLE AGAIN

TOM DOOLEY

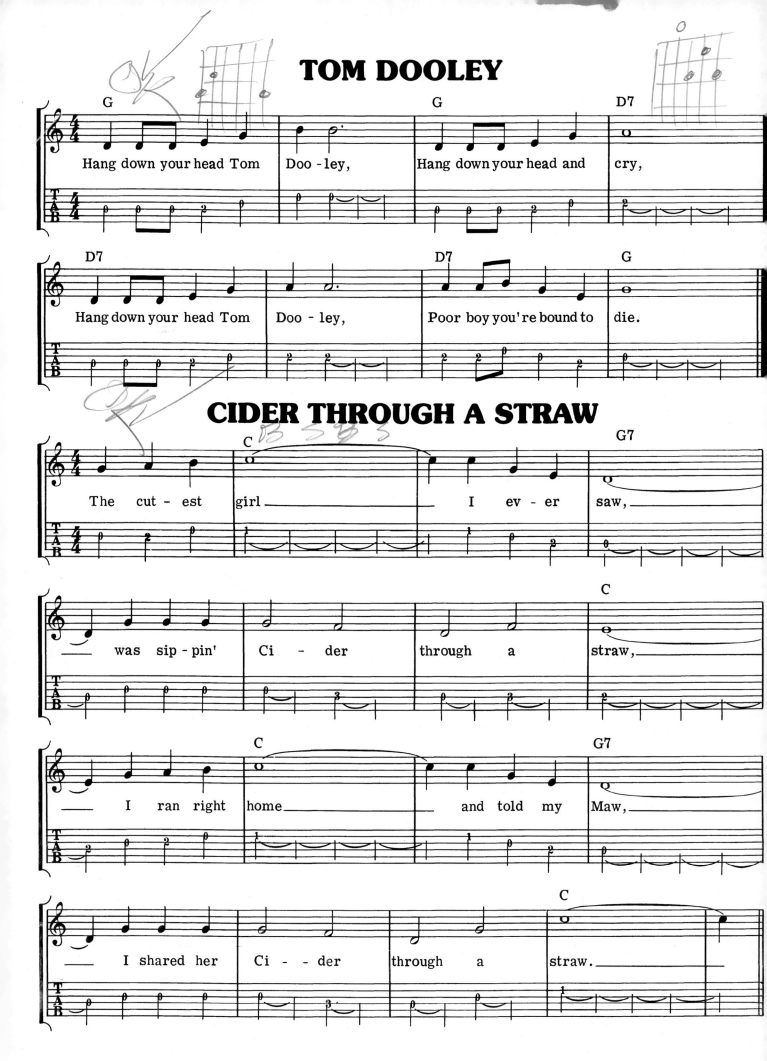

CIDER THROUGH A STRAW

24

♯ - This is a sharp. When placed before a note, play the note one fret higher.

SHARPING THE F'S

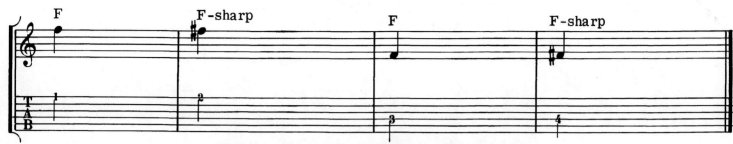

THE G MAJOR SCALE
(Practice Daily and Memorize)

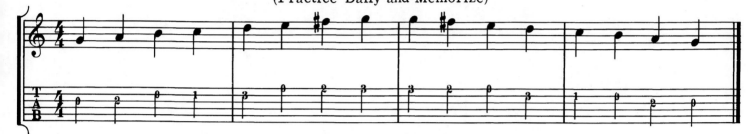

PLAYING THE LOW F SHARP

KEY SIGNATURE KEY OF G MAJOR

When a sharp is placed on the top line (F) of the music staff, this indicates the music is pitched in the G major scale and that all of the F's in the song are played as F♯'s. This is called the Key Signature. Other key signatures will be explained in detail later, but for now let's play some songs in the scale of G major.

YANKEE DOODLE

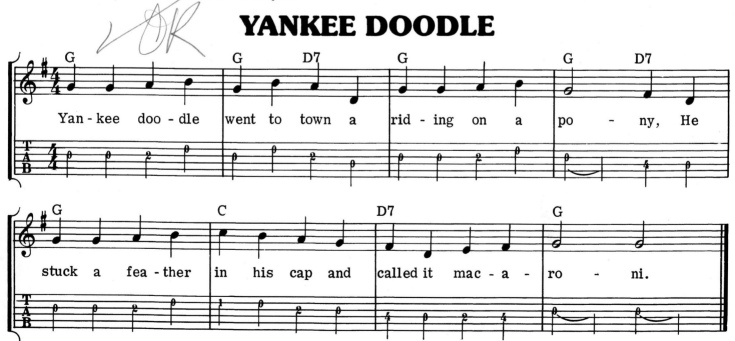

Yan - kee doo - dle went to town a rid - ing on a po - ny, He stuck a fea - ther in his cap and called it mac - a - ro - ni.

BUFFALO GALS

DOWN IN THE VALLEY

CLEMENTINE

NOTES ON THE "A" OR 5TH STRING

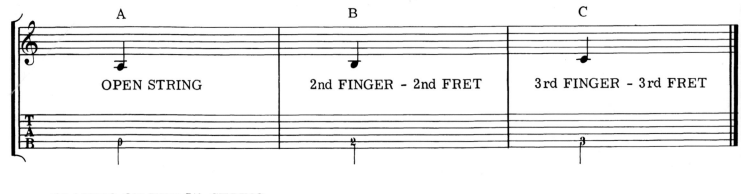

A — OPEN STRING

B — 2nd FINGER - 2nd FRET

C — 3rd FINGER - 3rd FRET

PLAYING ON THE 5th STRING

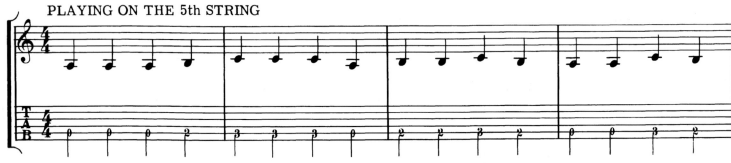

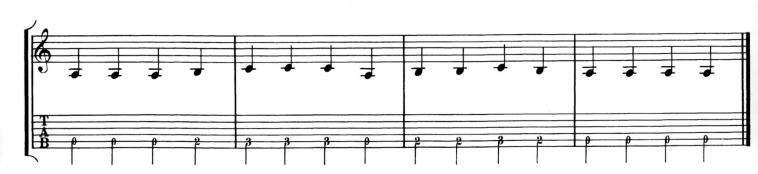

NOTE CHART

Below is a chart of all the notes you have learned - practice daily.

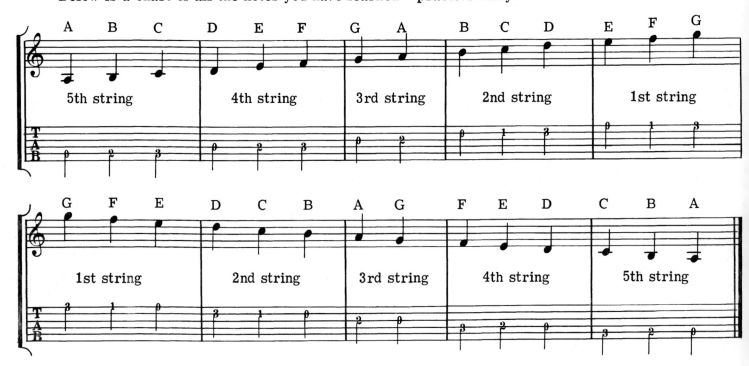

5th string — 4th string — 3rd string — 2nd string — 1st string

1st string — 2nd string — 3rd string — 4th string — 5th string

REUBEN, REUBEN

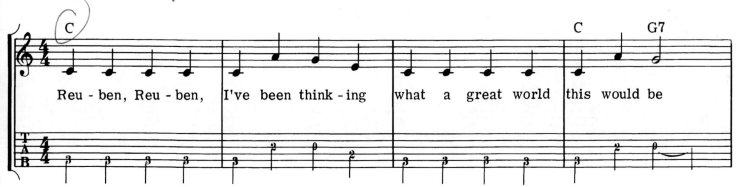

Reu - ben, Reu - ben, I've been think - ing what a great world this would be

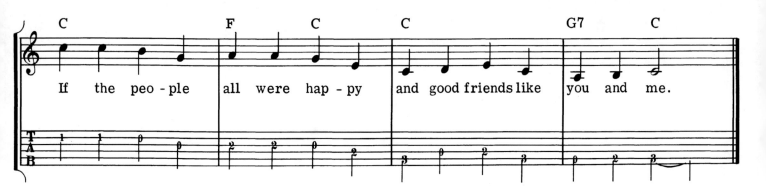

If the peo - ple all were hap - py and good friends like you and me.

WANDERING

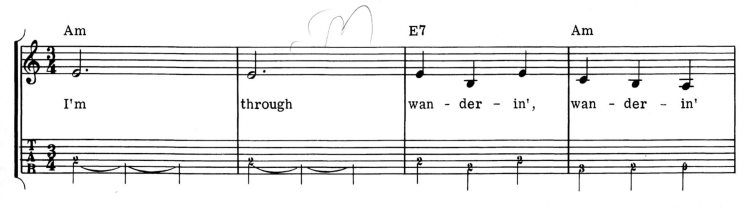

I'm through wan - der - in', wan - der - in'

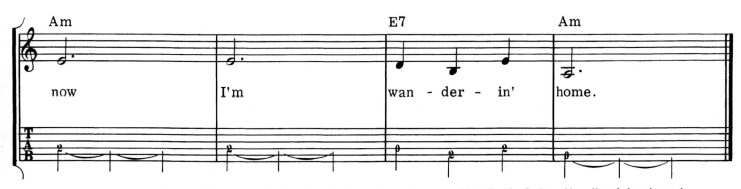

now I'm wan - der - in' home.

For thorough study into daily practice and technique building, see *Mel Bay's Guitar Handbook* book and companion stereo play-along cassette.

HARD, AIN'T IT HARD

NOTES ON THE "E" OR 6TH STRING

NOTE CHART

Below is a chart of all the notes you have learned - practice daily.

TURKEY IN THE STRAW

(Simplified)

HIGH "A" ON THE FIRST STRING

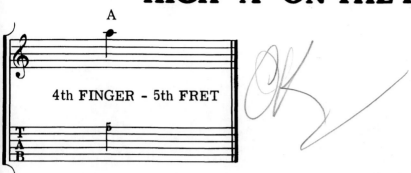

4th FINGER - 5th FRET

LONG, LONG AGO

Tell me the tales that to me were so dear,

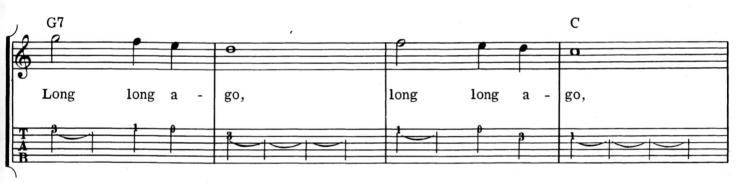

Long long a - go, long long a - go,

Sing me the song I de - light - ed to hear,

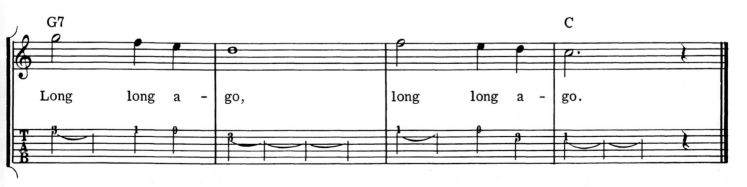

Long long a - go, long long a - go.

DOTTED QUARTER NOTE

A dot after a note increases its value by one-half of the original value.

EXERCISE USING DOTTED QUARTER NOTE

EXERCISE TWO

MICHAEL ROW THE BOAT ASHORE

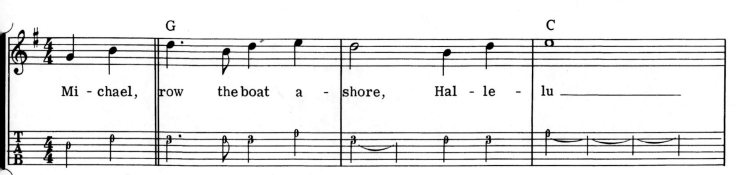

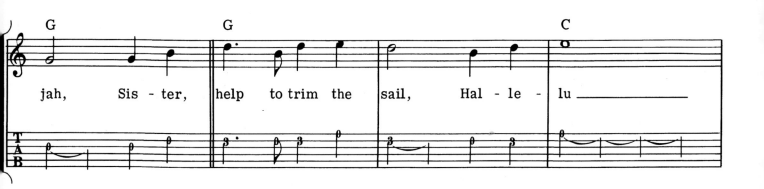

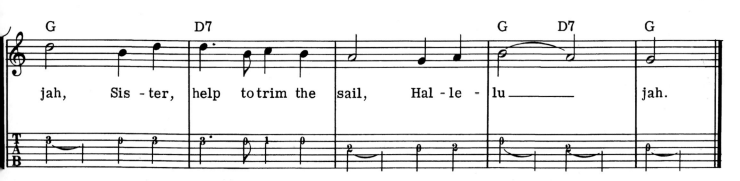

For thorough study into daily practice and technique building, see *Mel Bay's Guitar Handbook* book and companion stereo play-along cassette.

CHROMATICS

♯ sharps,   ♭ flats, and   ♮ naturals

The distance from one fret to the next is a half-step. Two half-steps make a whole step.

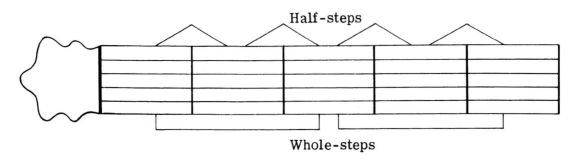

Note: From "open" to 1st fret is a half-step. From "open" to 2nd fret is a whole-step.

Half steps are one fret apart-Whole steps are two Frets apart.

Raising or lowering a tone is brought about by the use of the chromatic symbol:(♯-♭-♮)
These are also referred to as accidentals.

The Sharp ♯   The sharp placed before A note raises its pitch 1/2 step or one fret.

The Flat ♭   The flat placed before a note lowers its pitch 1/2 step or one fret.

The Natural ♮   The natural placed before a note restores the note to its
normal position-It cancels all accidentals used previously.

CHROMATIC NOTES — FIRST STRING

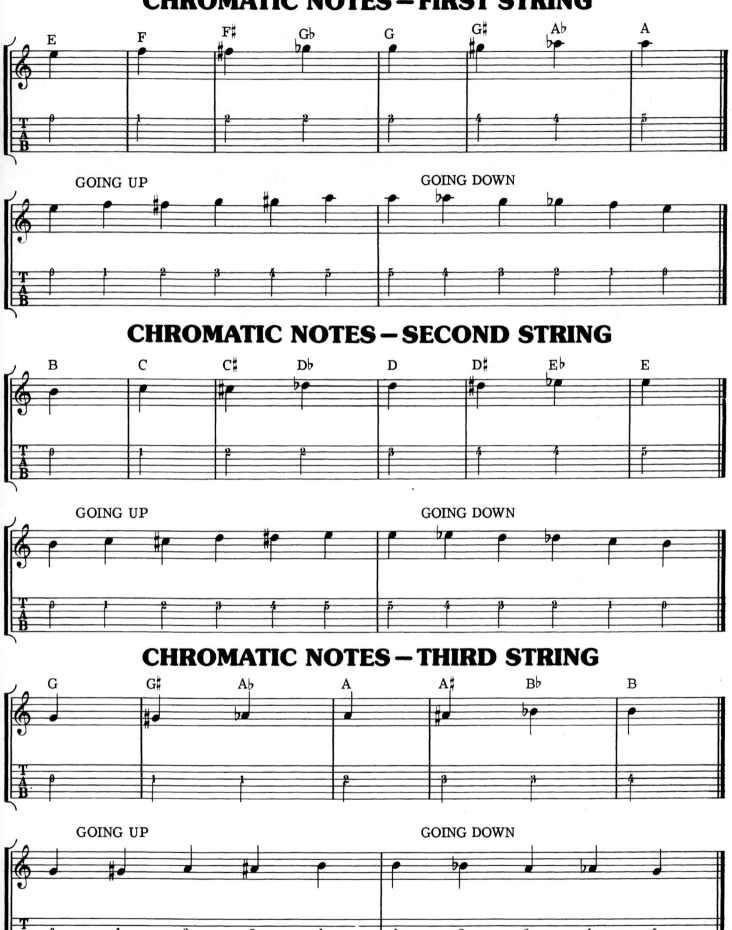

CHROMATIC NOTES — SECOND STRING

CHROMATIC NOTES — THIRD STRING

CHROMATIC NOTES — FOURTH STRING

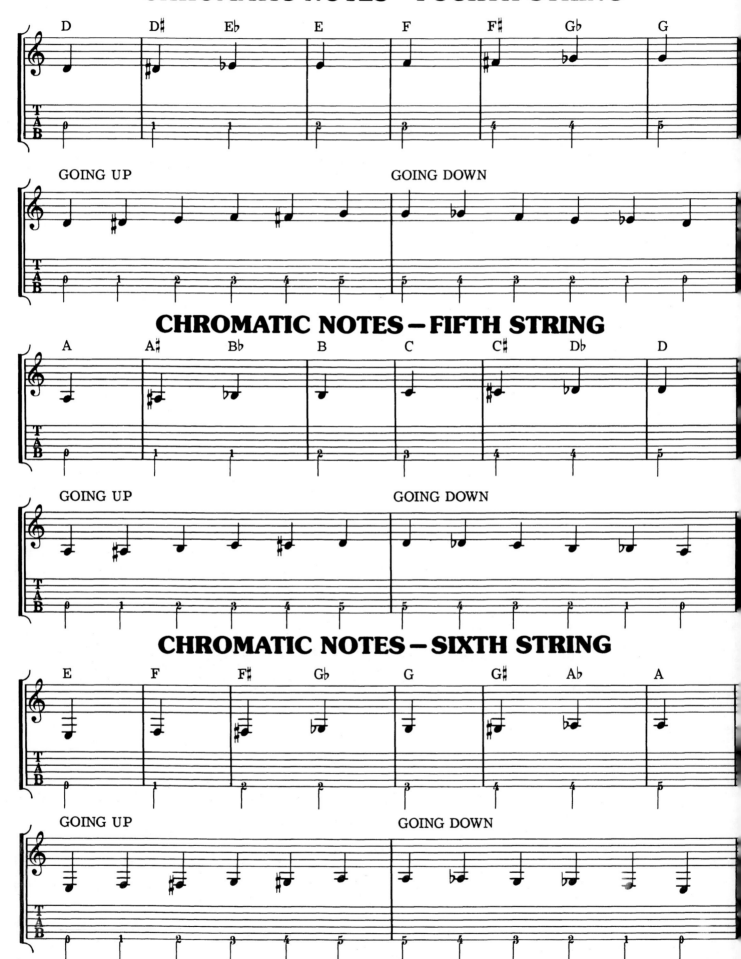

CHROMATIC NOTES — FIFTH STRING

CHROMATIC NOTES — SIXTH STRING

CHROMATIC SCALES

One octave chromatic scales as shown below use every halfstep within an octave.

THE C CHROMATIC SCALE

THE G CHROMATIC SCALE

THE D CHROMATIC SCALE

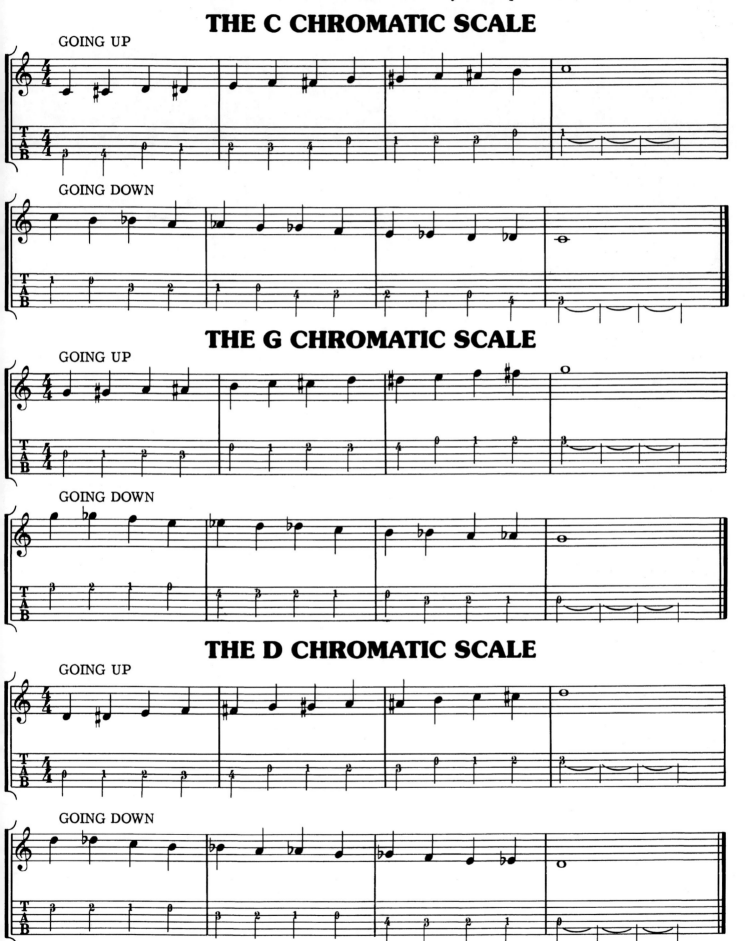

KEY SIGNATURES

Major Key Signatures

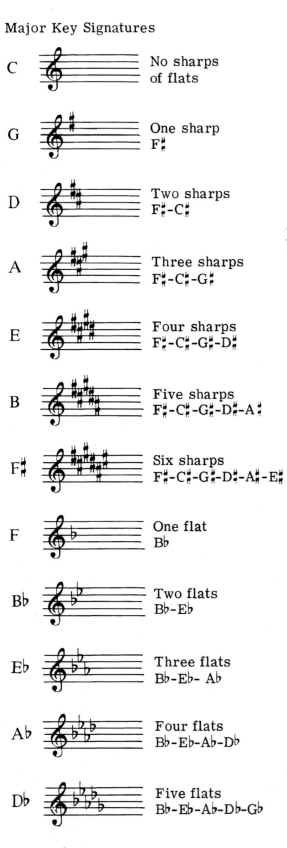

C — No sharps of flats

G — One sharp F♯

D — Two sharps F♯-C♯

A — Three sharps F♯-C♯-G♯

E — Four sharps F♯-C♯-G♯-D♯

B — Five sharps F♯-C♯-G♯-D♯-A♯

F♯ — Six sharps F♯-C♯-G♯-D♯-A♯-E♯

F — One flat B♭

B♭ — Two flats B♭-E♭

E♭ — Three flats B♭-E♭-A♭

A♭ — Four flats B♭-E♭-A♭-D♭

D♭ — Five flats B♭-E♭-A♭-D♭-G♭

G♭ — Six flats B♭-E♭-A♭-D♭-G♭-C♭

The Cycle of Keys

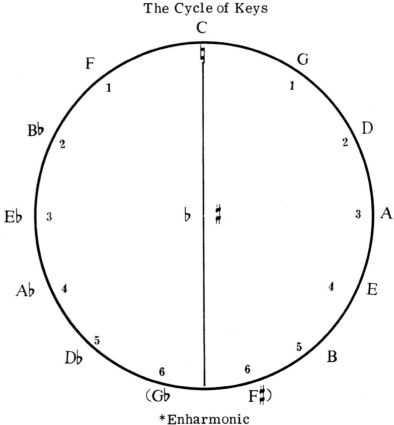

*Enharmonic

STARTING WITH C, MOVING TO THE RIGHT GIVES US THE KEYS CONTAINING SHARPS AND MOVING TO THE LEFT GIVES US THE KEYS CONTAINING FLATS.

*Enharmonic: Written differently as to notation but sounding the same.

TO FIND THE 3 MAIN CHORDS THAT ARE USED IN ANY KEY FIND THE NAME OF THE KEY ON THE ABOVE CIRCLE AND THAT WILL BE THE MAIN CHORD IN THAT KEY. THE OTHER 2 CHORDS ARE THE ONES SHOWN ON EACH SIDE OF THE MAIN CHORD. EXAMPLE: IN THE KEY OF D - D IS THE MAIN CHORD AND G AND A ARE THE OTHER TWO.

MEMORIZE THE KEY NAMES AND THE NUMBER OF SHARPS OR FLATS IN EACH KEY.

CHORD BACKGROUND

Playing the chord background is a very important part of Bluegrass guitar playing and a complete knowledge of chord playing is essential to learning the flat-picking style.

The section covers the two most popular ways to play chord background-chord strumming and bass-chord background.

Before attempting to play a song in the bluegrass flat-picking style, you should learn to pick out the tune in single note style as well as being able to play the chords that harmonize the tune as you will see as you go along, Bluegrass flat-picking is really a mixture of both.

Do not hurry through this material—study it carefully and learn it well. You cannot play well without it.

A chord is a group of three or more notes that blend beautifully together when played at the same time.

CHORD DIAGRAMS

A chord diagram is a drawing of the guitar neck. Hold the guitar in front of you so that you are facing the fingerboard (the smallest or 1st string should be on your right). Compare it to the drawing shown below.

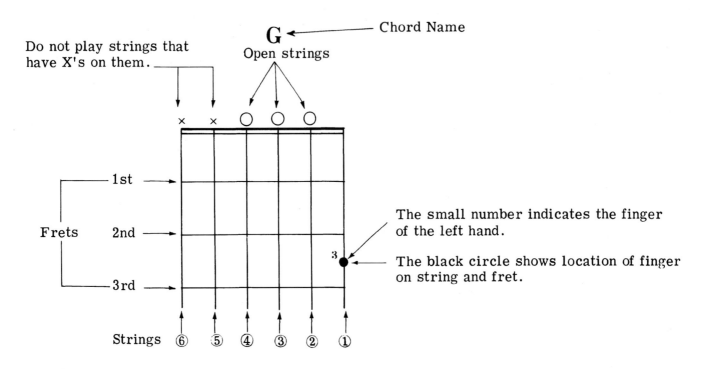

The vertical lines are the strings. The horizontal lines are the frets. The encircled numerals are the string numbers.

Open string = Do not touch string with the left hand.
    × = Do not pick string with the right hand.

HOW TO FINGER CHORDS

When making a chord, the fingers should be arched so the finger tips are pressing the strings straight in toward the finger board. Care should be taken that a finger does not touch any string other than the one it is depressing. The fingers should be placed firmly on the strings (as close to the frets as possible without getting directly on them.)

When two or three fingers of the left hand are used to form a chord, it is very improtant that you learn to put them all down at one time so that you will be able to change from one chord position to another quickly and smoothly.

> See Mel Bay's "Deluxe Encyclopedia of Guitar Chords"

THE BASIC CHORDS

There are many chords, but a thorough knowledge of the few basic ones shown is all you need to play the songs in this book as well as many others.

When you have learned how to use these chords for both strumming and bass-chord type playing we suggest you purchase a copy of Mel Bay's Deluxe Encylopedia of Guitar Chords. This will give you all the chords you will ever need to play any song in any key.

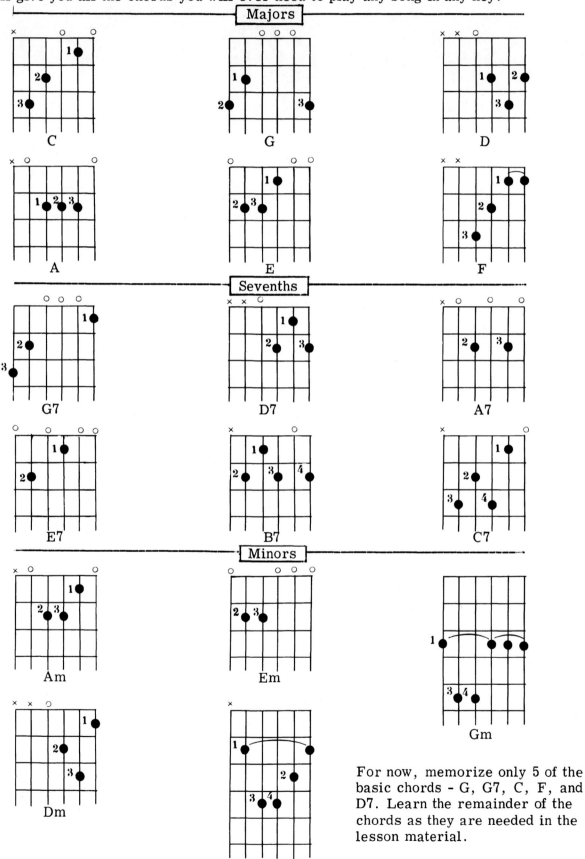

For now, memorize only 5 of the basic chords - G, G7, C, F, and D7. Learn the remainder of the chords as they are needed in the lesson material.

STRUMMING THE CHORDS

CHORD STRUMMING PROVIDES A PLEASANT RHYTHMIC BACKGROUND WHEN YOU SING A SONG OR WHEN SOMEONE ELSE PICKS THE TUNE ON ANOTHER INSTRUMENT. WE WILL NOW LEARN TO STRUM THREE BASIC CHORDS.

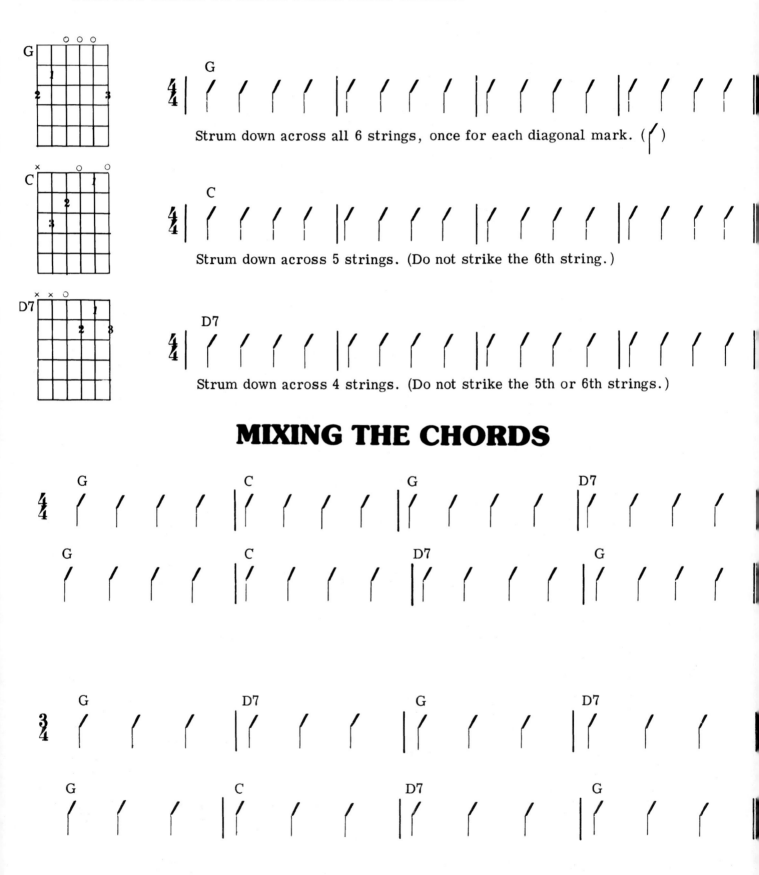

Strum down across all 6 strings, once for each diagonal mark. (╱)

Strum down across 5 strings. (Do not strike the 6th string.)

Strum down across 4 strings. (Do not strike the 5th or 6th strings.)

MIXING THE CHORDS

DOWN AND UP STRUMMING

So far we have used only down strums ___ one on each count of each measure. For more rapid strums, we add the up strum.

When strumming two times to each count we strum down and then immediately back up. (↓) means down strum and (↑) means up strum.

The stems on the diagonal chord lines indicate the time given each chord in exactly the same manner as they do on the notes.

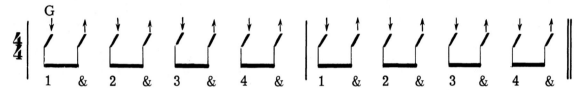

When strumming in half-counts, always strum down on the first half-count and up on the last half-count.

Many songs will use a mixture of strums. Here are a few examples:

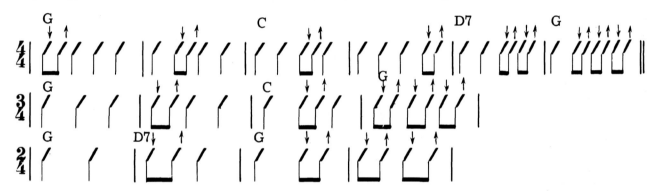

Remember, the quarter note or one count strum (⟋) will always be strummed down. The eighth note or half-count strums (⟋⟋) will always be strummed down for the first half-count and up for the second half-count.

IF YOU UNDERSTAND THIS STRUMMING SYSTEM AND YOU LEARN ALL OF THE BASIC CHORDS YOU SHOULD BE ABLE TO STRUM ALL OF THE SONGS IN THIS BOOK PLUS MANY OTHERS.

Many song books you can purchase use the system you have just learned to show the proper chord strums but regular piano-vocal sheet music and other song books just show the name of the chords above the music's melody. When the chord strums are not shown as above, simply strum one chord for each count of the measure. (The top number of the time signature always tells you how many times to strum in each measure.)

YOU SHOULD GO BACK NOW AND PRACTICE STRUMMING THE CHORDS TO ALL THE SONGS YOU HAVE LEARNED TO PLAY SO FAR. REMEMBER, YOU CAN NOT ALWAYS BE THE SOLO PLAYER. IT IS VERY IMPORTANT TO KNOW HOW TO PLAY THE CHORD PART WHEN SOMEONE IS CARRYING THE MELODY ON ANOTHER INSTRUMENT. IN ORDER TO PLAY PROFICIENTLY, YOU MUST BE ABLE TO CHANGE CHORDS FIRMLY AND QUICKLY.

Remember: In 4/4 time you strum 4 chords in each measure. In 3/4 time strum 3 etc.

For thorough study into daily practice and technique building, see *Mel Bay's Guitar Handbook* book and companion stereo play-along cassette.

SOLO STYLE—MELODY AND CHORDS TOGETHER

THE FIRST STEP IN LEARNING TO PICK IN THE FLAT-PICKING BLUEGRASS STYLE
IS TO LEARN TO MIX THE NOTES AND CHORDS RAPIDLY. IN THE NEXT TWO SONGS
YOU PICK BOTH THE NOTES IN THE MELODY AND THE CHORDS SO THAT THE
SOUND OF THE SONGS WILL BE COMPLETE.

GOOD NIGHT LADIES

BILE' DEM CABBAGE DOWN

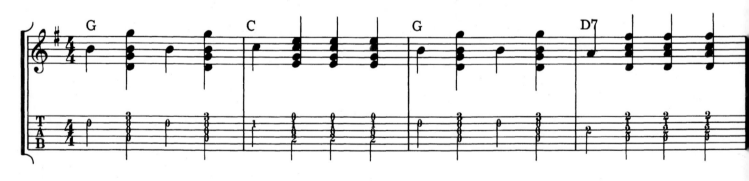

46

SOLO FLAT—PICKING USING DOUBLE-STRUMS

THE RHYTHMIC-GALLOPING SOUND THAT IS SO COMMON IN THE FLAT-PICKING STYLE IS ACCOMPLISHED BY THE USE OF RAPID DOWN AND UP STRUMMING OF THE CHORDS IN THE SOLOS. LET'S PLAY THE LAST TWO SONGS AGAIN, BUT THIS TIME THERE ARE TWO CHORDS ($\frac{1}{2}$ count each) TO EACH BEAT INSTEAD OF ONE.

GOOD NIGHT LADIES

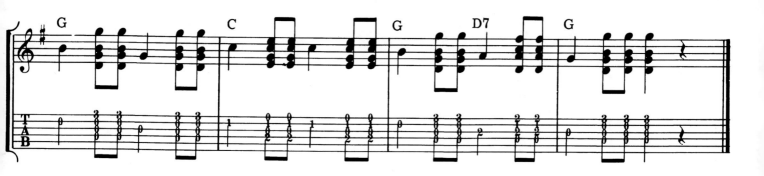

BILE' DEM CABBAGE DOWN

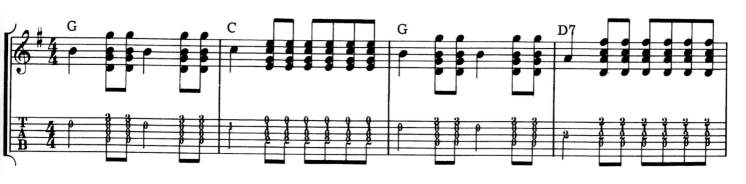

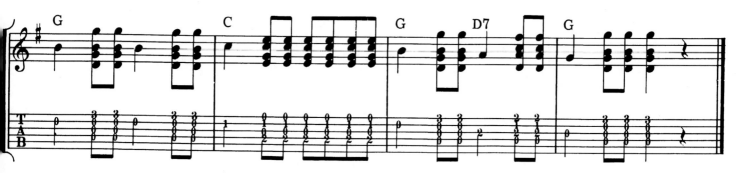

BASS NOTES AND ALTERNATE BASS NOTES
MAJOR CHORDS

In Bluegrass Solo and Background Picking, bass notes and alternate bass notes are used to dress up the sound and give an effect like a Bass Player added to the chords. Shown below are examples of this type of playing.

In the diagrams below: ■ = Bass Note (Pushed Down)   □ = Bass Note (Open)

▲ = Alternate Bass Note (Pushed Down)   △ = Alternate Bass Note (Open)

48

BASS NOTES AND ALTERNATE BASS NOTES
SEVENTH CHORDS

BASS NOTES AND ALTERNATE BASS NOTES
MINOR CHORDS

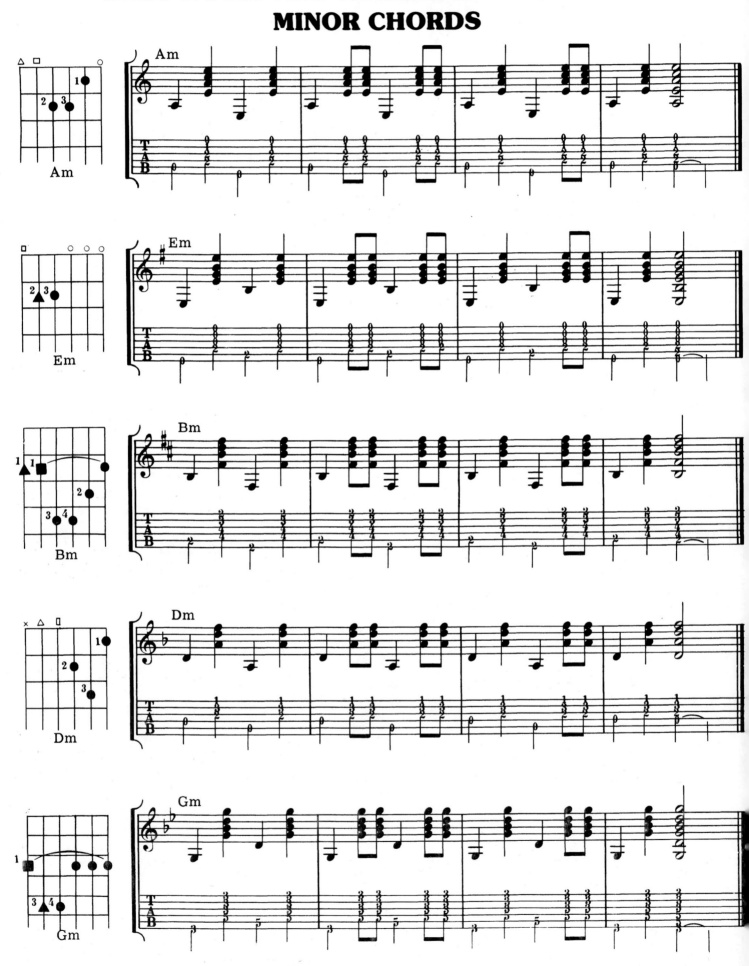

BASS RUNS

Bass runs are usually made up of passing tones between the chords. They can be used to lead into new phrases or different sections, such as verse into chorus.

Bass runs can often be played one measure before a chord change. The following example illustrates this bass-run formula in the key of G major.

BASS RUNS IN G MAJOR

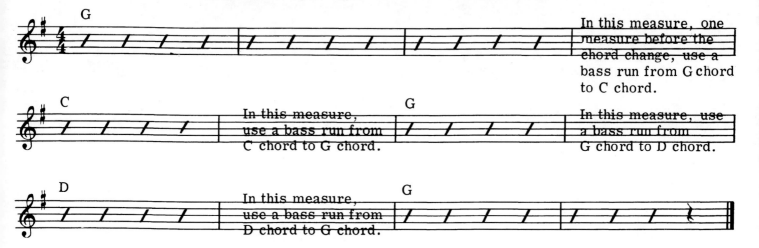

Now, let's play the above progression using the alternate bass technique with bass runs one measure before a chord change.

51

BASS RUNS IN C MAJOR

Below is the bass-run formula for the key of C major.

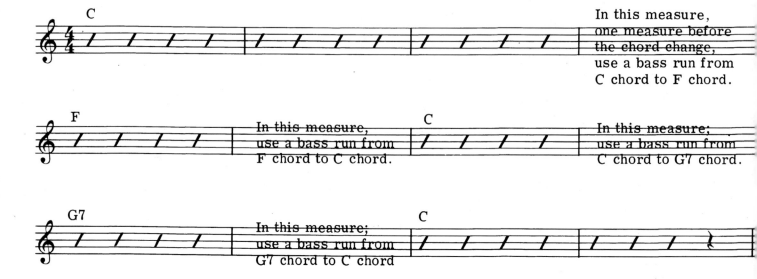

Now, let's use the alternate bass technique with bass runs one measure before a chord change - in the key of C major.

CONNECTING BASS RUNS

Bass Runs are usually made up of scale notes between the chords. They can be used to lead into new phrases, connect chords, or ending a section.

Playing the example below in numerical order (1 thru 12) will give you a better idea of the sound when connecting one chord to another within a song.

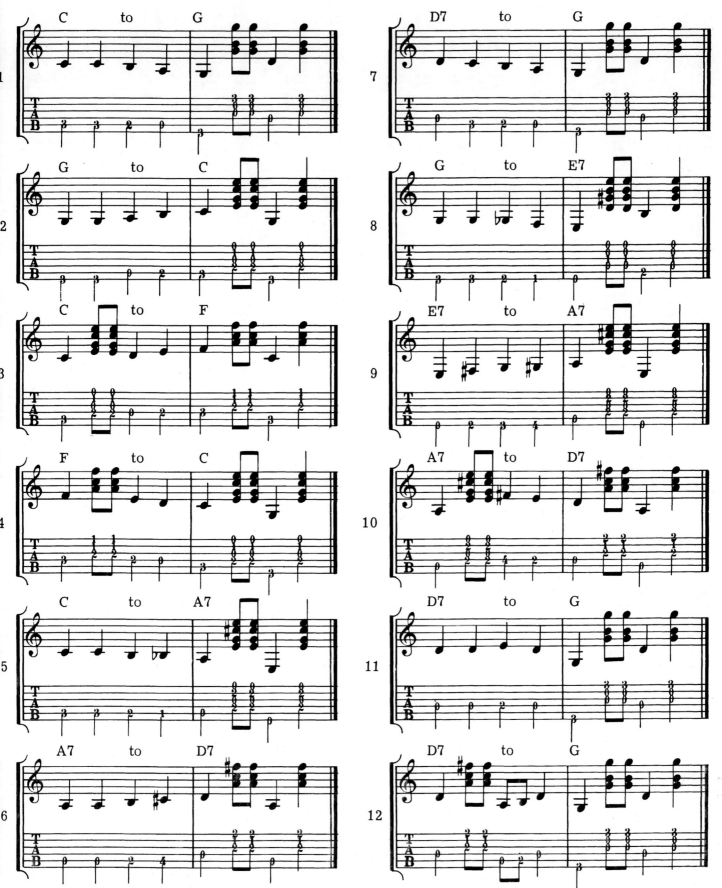

COUNTING REVIEW

MIXING AND COUNTING THE DIFFERENT NOTE VALUES

Count aloud as you play - you must go slow and steady.

FLAT PICKING TECHNIQUE SECTION

Do not attempt to play any of the full flat-picking solos until you have mastered the following:

THE HAMMER

THE PULL-OFF

THE SLIDE

FILLS AND
ENDINGS

THE CAPO

THE HAMMER

Our first bluegrass effect is the hammer. To perform the hammer, pick the first note in the normal way. To obtain the second note, tap the left hand finger down hard and fast onto the string from about an inch above the fingerboard. Hammering right behind a fret gives the clearest and loudest sound.

In the Hammer example below, you pick the string only once but two separate notes are sounded. Always pick the first note a little harder when hammering so that both notes will be heard clearly before the sound dies away.

HAMMER EXAMPLE

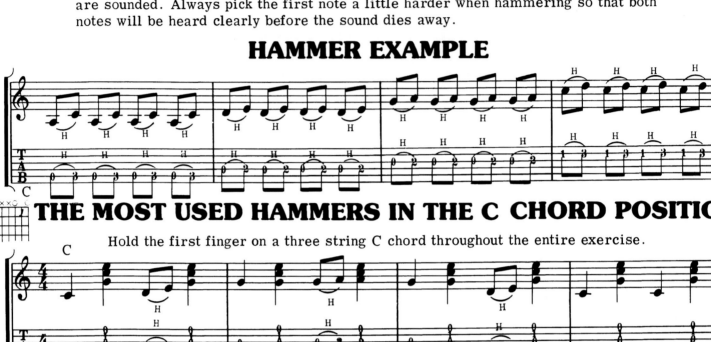

THE MOST USED HAMMERS IN THE C CHORD POSITIO

Hold the first finger on a three string C chord throughout the entire exercise.

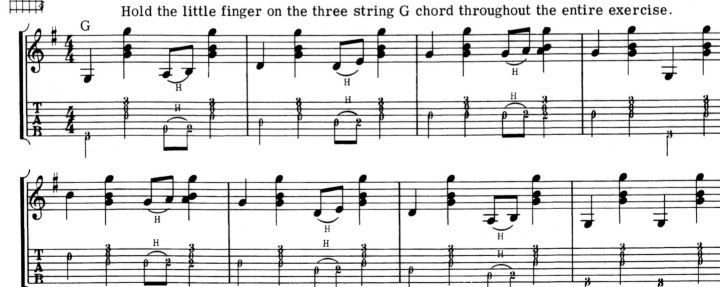

THE MOST USED HAMMERS IN THE G CHORD POSITIO

Hold the little finger on the three string G chord throughout the entire exercise.

Repeat the above exercise using a three string G7 chord instead of the G chord.

THE PULL OFF

The next effect we will learn is the pull-off. To perform the pull-off, pick the first note in the normal way. To obtain the second note use the left hand finger you are pushing the string down with to "pluck" or pick the string in a downward direction. The sound will be clearer if you keep pressure on the string as you pull-off the left hand finger.

As in the hammer, pick the first note a little harder so that both notes will be heard clearly before the sound dies away.

PULL-OFF EXAMPLE

THE MOST USED PULL-OFFS IN THE C CHORD POSITION

Hold the first finger on the three string C chord throughout the entire exercise.

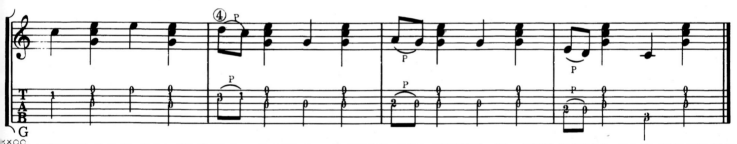

THE MOST USED PULL-OFFS IN THE G CHORD POSITION

Hold the little finger on the three string G chord throughout the entire exercise.

THE SLIDE

To perform the slide, another effect used in bluegrass guitar playing, pick the first note in the normal way, then keeping the left hand finger pressed firmly down, slide quickly to the second note which is found in the fret shown in the tablature.

As in the hammer and the pull-off, pick the first note a little harder so that both notes will be heard clearly before the sound dies away.

SLIDE EXAMPLE

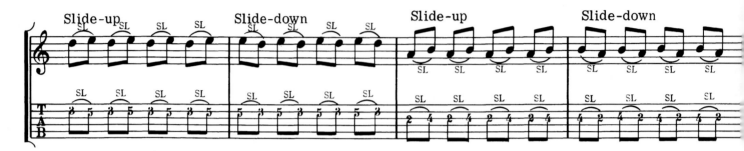

THE MOST USED SLIDES IN THE KEY OF C

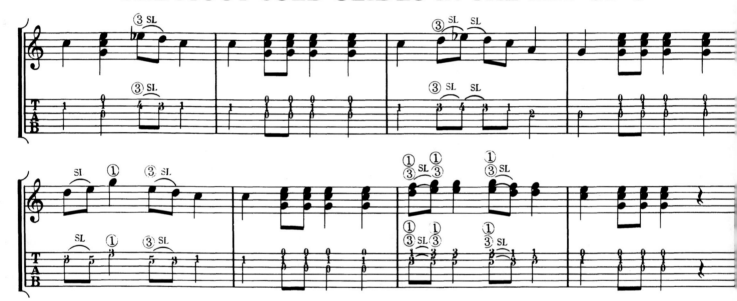

THE MOST USED SLIDES IN THE KEY OF G

FILLS AND ENDINGS

When a melody note is held for several counts, usually four to six counts, fills are
used. Below are a number of fills in the keys of G and C.

KEY OF G

KEY OF C

FILLS AND ENDINGS

FILLS AND ENDINGS

KEY OF G

KEY OF C

61

THE CAPO

THE CAPO IS A DEVICE THAT CLAMPS AROUND THE NECK OF THE GUITAR AT ANY FRET AND PRESSES DOWN ALL SIX STRINGS AT ONE TIME THERE BY ESTABLISHING A NEW TUNING.

THE USE OF THE CAPO ENABLES YOU TO PLAY IN OTHER MUSICAL KEYS, STILL USING THE SAME BASIC CHORD FORMATIONS THAT YOU HAVE LEARNED. EACH TIME THE CAPO IS RAISED ONE FRET IT HAS THE EFFECT OF TUNING THE GUITAR ONE HALF-STEP HIGHER.

THE TWO MOST POPULAR TYPES OF GUITAR CAPOS ARE METAL AND ELASTIC. WE RECCOMEND THE ELASTIC TYPE AS IT WILL NOT SCRATCH THE NECK OF THE GUITAR.

THE GUITAR CAN BE PLAYED IN ANY KEY WITHOUT THE USE OF A CAPO BUT IT IS VERY USEFUL IN BLUEGRASS FLATPICKING SO THAT YOU CAN MAINTAIN THAT "OPEN STRING" SOUND.

THE FOLLOWING CHART SHOWS WHAT CHORDS ARE OBTAINED BY USING THE BASIC CHORD POSITIONS AND PLACING THE CAPO IN THE FIRST FIVE FRETS.

THE TYPE OF CHORD YOU START WITH IS THE TYPE YOU WILL OBTAIN AS YOU MOVE UP. FOR INSTANCE IS YOU START WITH AN OPEN "G" CHORD IT WILL BECOME AN "A♭" CHORD WHEN THE CAPO IS IN THE FIRST FRET --- IF YOU START WITH AN OPEN "G7" CHORD IT WILL BECOME AN "A♭7" CHORD ETC.

CAPO TRANSPOSITION CHART

TO USE THE CHART BELOW SIMPLY FIND THE KEY THE MUSIC IS WRITTEN IN ON THE TOP LINE. (IF YOU ARE NOT SURE WHAT KEY YOU ARE IN REFER TO PAGE 40 AND COMPARE THE KEY SIGNATURE - NUMBER OF SHARPS OR FLATS). FIND THE KEY YOU WANT TO CHANGE TO BY LOOKING DOWN THE COLUMN DIRECTLY UNDER THE KEY CHORD AND PLACE THE CAPO IN THE FRET INDICATED ON THE LEFT OF THE CHART. PLAY THE SONG EXACTLY AS YOU WOULD WITHOUT THE CAPO AND YOU WILL BE PLAYING IN THE NEW KEY.

Letter Name of Basic open chord	G	A	B	C	D	E	F
With capo in 1st fret becomes	A♭	B♭	C	D♭	E♭	F	F♯
With capo in 2nd fret becomes	A	B	C♯	D	E	F♯	G
With capo in 3rd fret becomes	B♭	C	D	E♭	F	G	A♭
With capo in 4th fret becomes	B	C♯	E♭	E	F♯	A♭	A
With capo in 5th fret becomes	C	D	E	F	G	A	B♭

For thorough study into daily practice and technique building, see *Mel Bay's Guitar Handbook* book and companion stereo play-along cassette.

SOLO SECTION

Every solo is written twice in this solo section. Once in simple form showing the tune, the words, and the chords and once in the full flat-picking style. You should be able to play the simple versions of all the songs when you have completed the sections covering reading music and chord strumming

Do not attempt to play the flat-picking solos until you have mastered the section on Bluegrass effects.

When you have learned to play the flat-picking solos, the simple versions that match can be used for accompaniment by any other chord playing instrument.

INDEX

You will notice that left hand finger numbers have been placed over some of the notes in the flat-picking solos. Although these are shown in the tablature, they are there to remind you which way is correct when there is a choice of where that particular note can be played.

OLD TIME RELIGION

Gimme that old time re - li - gion, Gimme that old time re - li - gion, Gimme that old time re - li - gion, It's good e - nough for me, It was good for the He - brew child - ren, It was good for the He - brew child - ren, It was good for the He — brew child -ren, It's good e -nough for me.

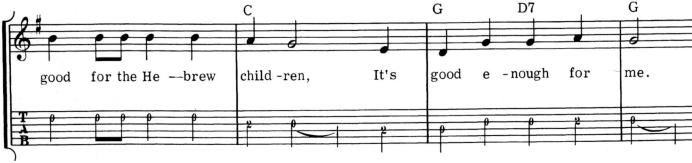

OLD TIME RELIGION

BILE' DEM CABBAGE DOWN

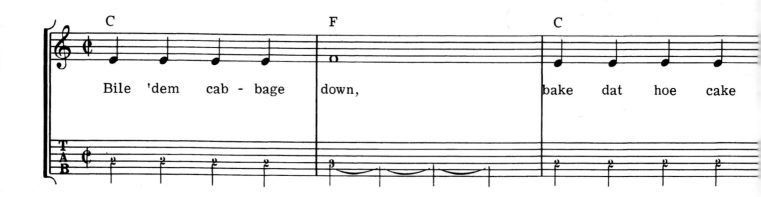

Bile 'dem cab-bage down, down, bake dat hoe cake

brown, the on-ly song that I can sing is

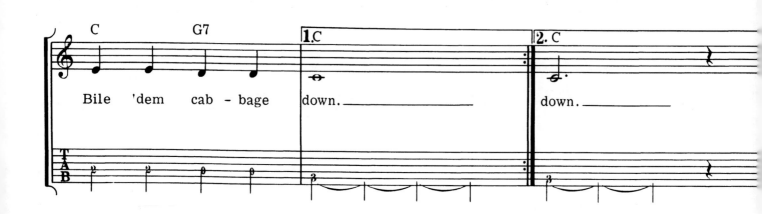

Bile 'dem cab-bage down._____ down._____

BILE' DEM CABBAGE DOWN

OLD DAN TUCKER

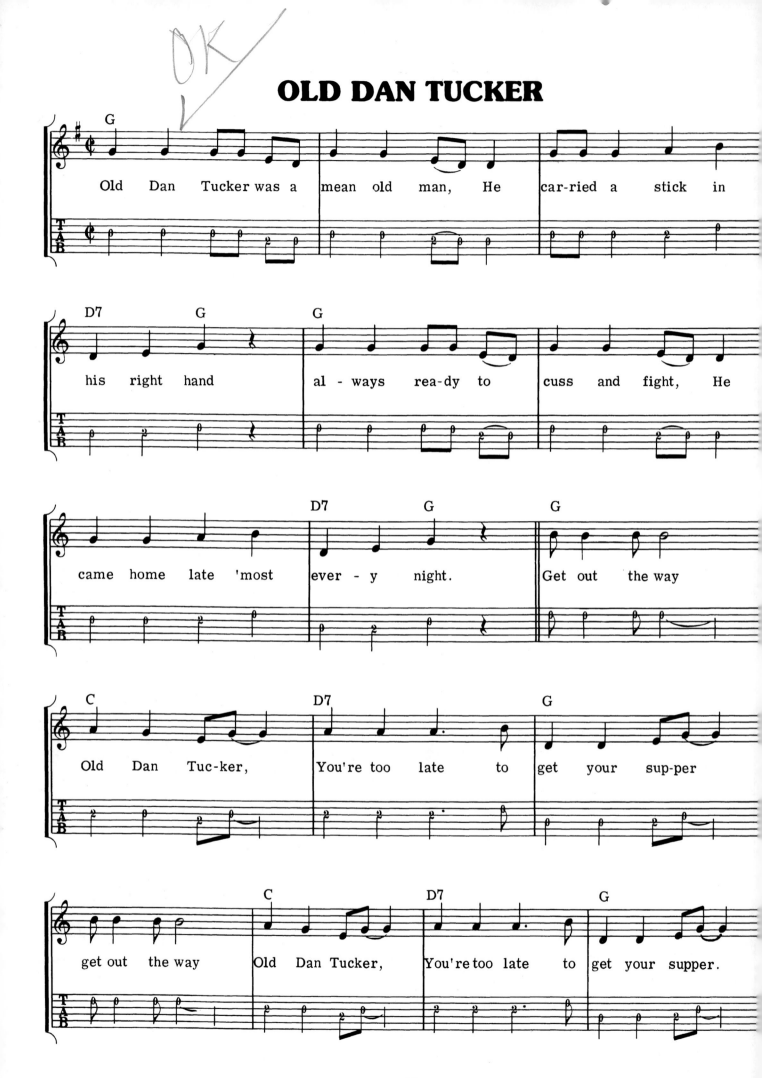

Old Dan Tucker was a mean old man, He car-ried a stick in his right hand al - ways rea-dy to cuss and fight, He came home late 'most ever - y night. Get out the way Old Dan Tuc-ker, You're too late to get your sup-per get out the way Old Dan Tucker, You're too late to get your supper.

OLD DAN TUCKER

CARELESS LOVE

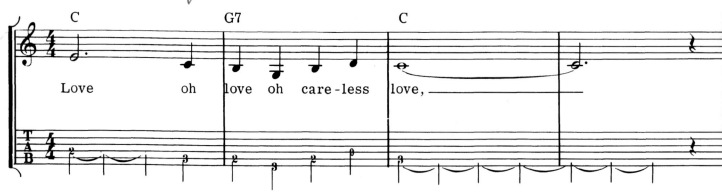

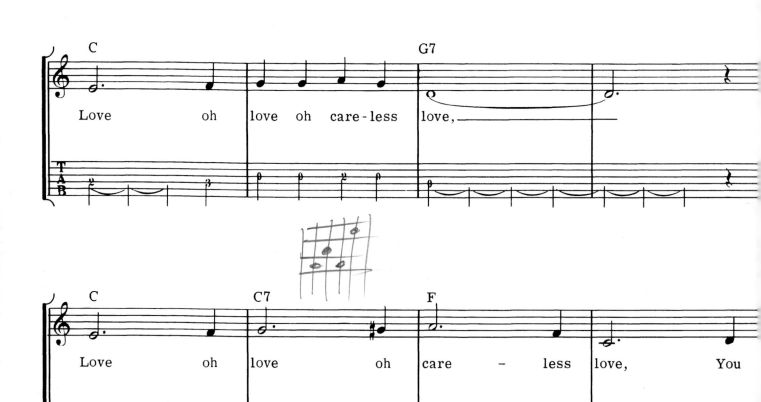

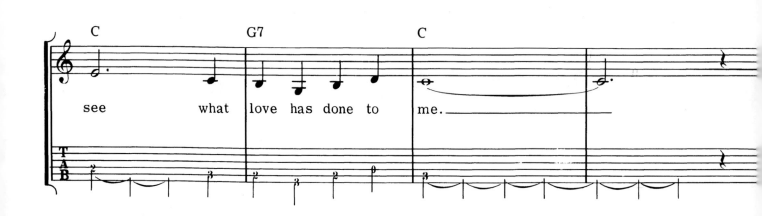

CARELESS LOVE

RED RIVER VALLEY

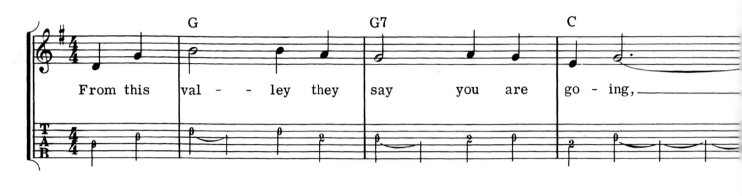

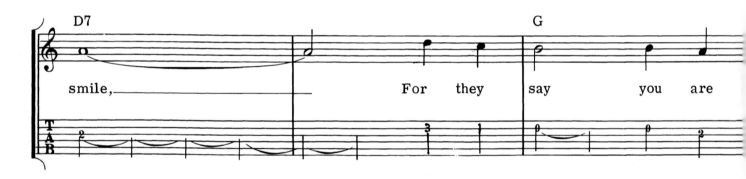

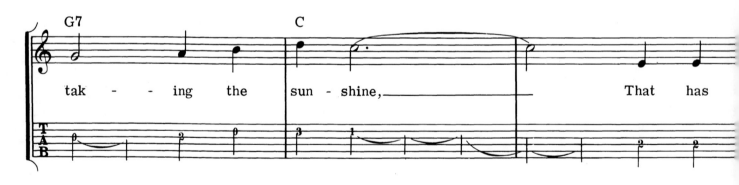

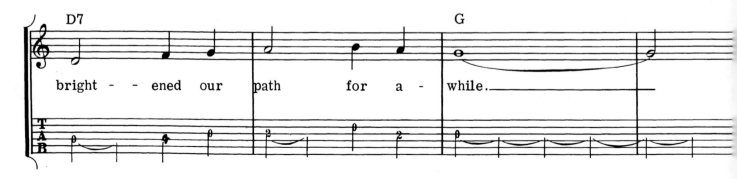

RED RIVER VALLEY

CRIPPLE CREEK

CRIPPLE CREEK

LEAN ON JESUS

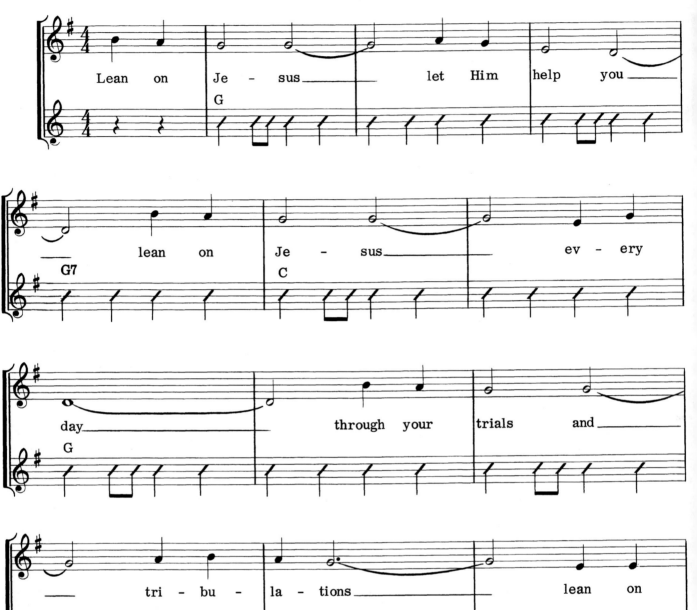

Lean on Je - sus ___ let Him help you ___
___ lean on Je - sus ___ ev - ery
day ___ through your trials and ___
___ tri - bu - la - tions ___ lean on
Je - sus all the way ___

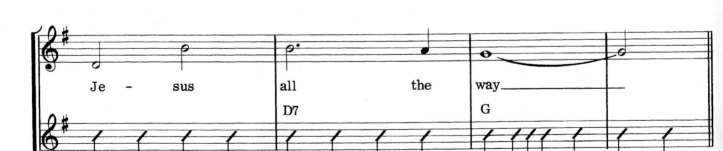

2. Walk with Jesus etc.
3. Talk to Jesus etc.
4. Live for Jesus etc.

LEAN ON JESUS

For thorough study into daily practice and technique building, see *Mel Bay's Guitar Handbook* book and companion stereo play-along cassette.

CINDY

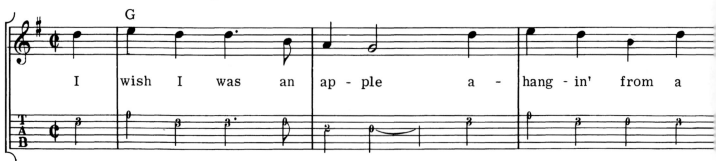

I wish I was an ap - ple a - hang - in' from a

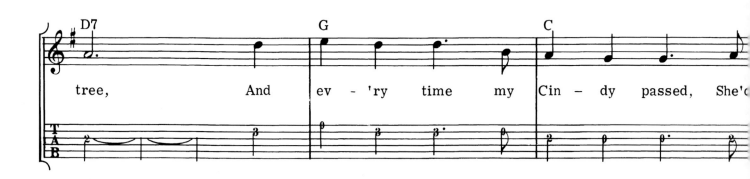

tree, And ev - 'ry time my Cin - dy passed, She'd

take a bite of me, Get a - long home, Cin - dy,

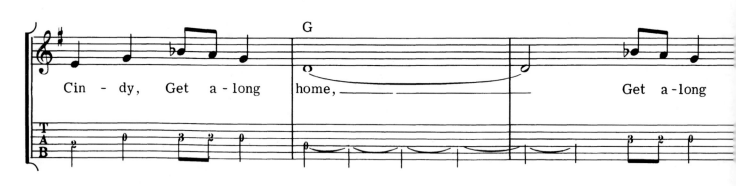

Cin - dy, Get a - long home, _____ Get a - long

home, Cin - dy, Cin - dy, I'll mar - ry you some day.

CINDY

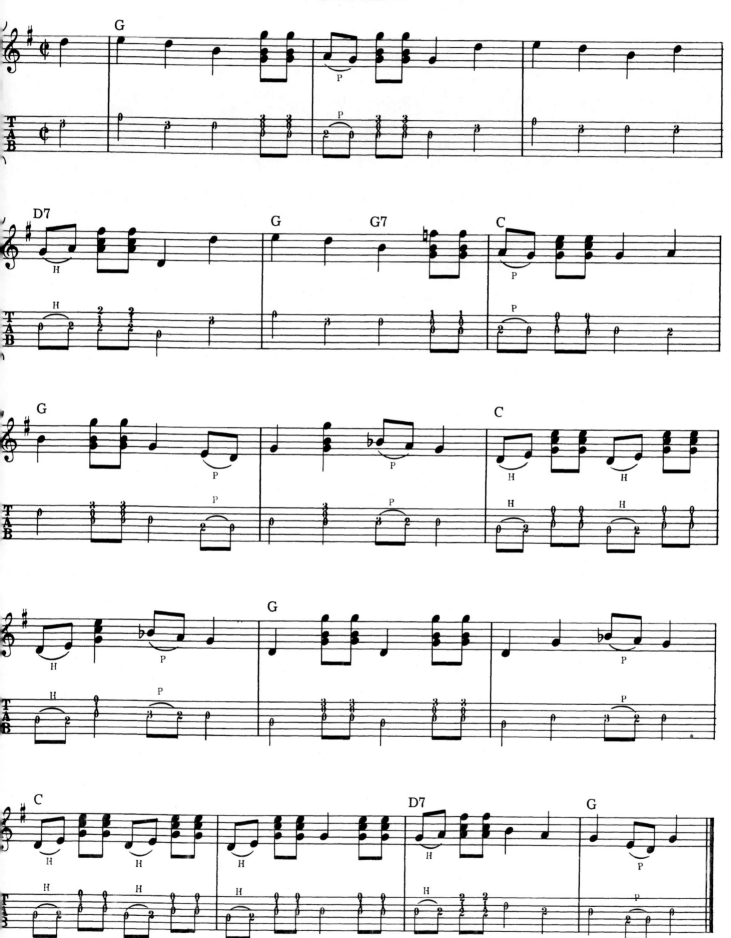

79

SHE'LL BE COMING 'ROUND THE MOUNTAIN

SHE'LL BE COMING 'ROUND THE MOUNTAIN

MAMA DON'T 'LOW

MAMA DON'T 'LOW

HAND ME DOWN MY WALKING CANE

HAND ME DOWN MY WALKING CANE

OLD JOE CLARK

OLD JOE CLARK

BUFFALO GALS

BUFFALO GALS

WILDWOOD FLOWER

WILDWOOD FLOWER

91

BANKS OF THE OHIO

BANKS OF THE OHIO

WRECK OF THE OLD 97

Oh they gave him his or - ders at Mon - roe Vir - gin - ia, say - ing "Steve, you're way be hind time,_____ this is not Thir - ty Eight, But it's Old Nine - ty Sev - en, Got to get her in - to Spen - cer on time."_____

WRECK OF THE OLD 97

ARKANSAS TRAVELER

Traditional Melody
Words by Neil Griffin

ARKANSAS TRAVELER

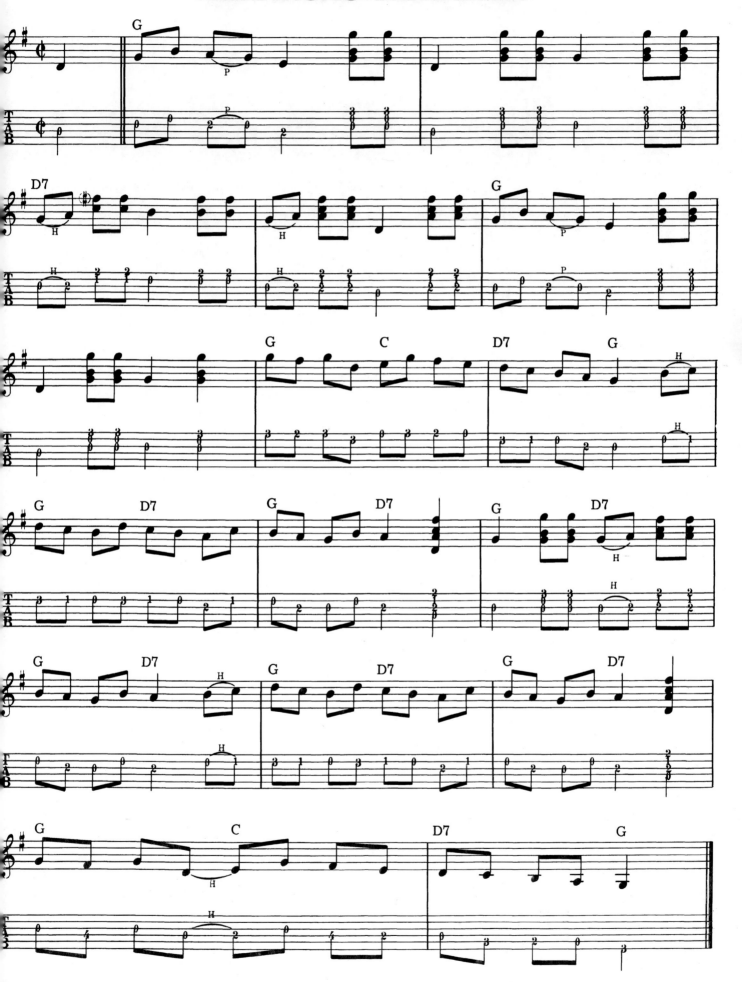

JOHN HENRY

JOHN HENRY

SOURWOOD MOUNTAIN

SOURWOOD MOUNTAIN

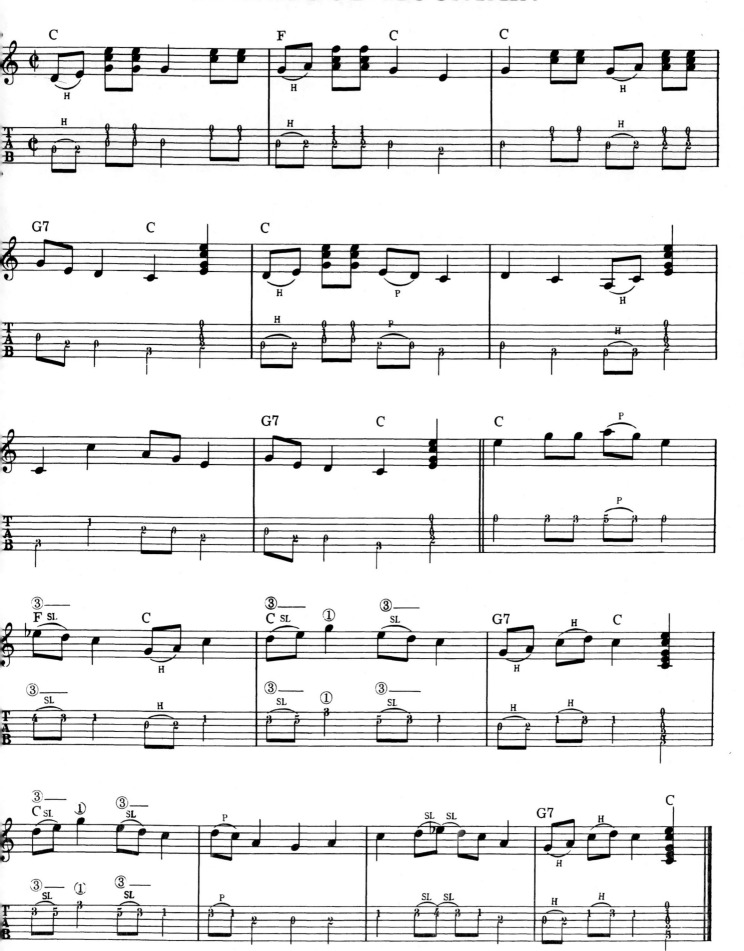

NEIL'S REEL

By Neil Grif

GOLDEN SLIPPERS

LIBERTY